Original title:
Shadows of Elsewhere

Copyright © 2024 Creative Arts Management OÜ
All rights reserved.

Author: Riley Donovan
ISBN HARDBACK: 978-9916-90-720-7
ISBN PAPERBACK: 978-9916-90-721-4

Dreams Laced with Melancholy

In shadows cast by fading light,
Whispers of the past take flight.
Each wish once bright now cloaked in gray,
A heart's lament, the price we pay.

Through silver clouds, memories drift,
Carrying hopes, a fragile gift.
Yet in the sorrow, beauty lies,
A dance of tears, where silence cries.

Phantoms of the Imagination

In corners dark where dreams reside,
Phantoms wander, and thoughts collide.
Visions swirl in midnight's bloom,
Painting shadows upon the gloom.

With whispered tales of what could be,
They offer glimpses, setting free.
Yet fear and hope both intertwine,
Creating worlds that blur the line.

Wandering Through the Echo Chamber

Lost in a maze of words we weave,
Each voice a thought we can't believe.
Reflections dance on polished glass,
Where moments meld and shadows pass.

In chambers wide, opinions clash,
Resonating with each loud crash.
Yet truth remains a distant star,
Guiding us through realms bizarre.

Reflections of Lost Journeys

On winding paths where echoes fade,
We trace the steps that time has made.
Each sigh a story left untold,
In twilight's glow, the heart feels cold.

With every turn, a chance to find,
Fragments of the past entwined.
In quiet moments, we receive,
The lessons learned, the dreams we weave.

Riddles of the Vanished Grove

Whispers weave through ancient trees,
Secrets held in the cool, soft breeze.
Footsteps echo, then fade away,
In the stillness of the dying day.

A flicker of light, a shiver of sound,
Mysteries dance on sacred ground.
What was lost, and what remains?
In the shadows, knowledge reigns.

Fables from Beyond the Gloom

In the corners where shadows play,
Legends breathe, then slip away.
Tales of love, and hopes that ache,
Stories forged in dreams we make.

A mirror reflects a world unknown,
Where whispers of fate are overthrown.
In the depths of a curling mist,
Lies the truth that none can resist.

Illusions of a Hidden Place

Veils of fog hide what is near,
Echoes of laughter, draped in fear.
What is real, and what is dreamed?
In the light of doubt, all is redeemed.

Through the brambles, a path unfolds,
Woven stories of the brave and bold.
Each step whispers, 'Seek and find,'
In this realm, all is intertwined.

Chronicles of the Dim-lit Way

Paths entwined with shadows deep,
Guided by the stars we keep.
Every turn reveals a sign,
Hints of fate in the intertwine.

Days drift in a soft embrace,
Moments linger, time can't erase.
In the hush of twilight's call,
Echoes linger, revealing all.

The Dance of Unseen Hours

In shadows where the moments fade,
Time twirls softly, a silent cascade.
Whispers echo in twilight's embrace,
As dreams waltz in a timeless space.

Beneath the stars that gently gleam,
Unseen hours weave a tender dream.
Memories linger in the night's song,
Where fleeting seconds have belonged.

Glimmers of What Once Was

Golden echoes from days long past,
Shimmer like dewdrops, fading fast.
In the silence, stories ignite,
Glimmers of hope in the soft twilight.

With every breath, nostalgia swells,
Faint laughter ringing like distant bells.
Through the haze of forgotten lore,
Lives a spark we can't ignore.

Voices from the Winding Path

Along the trail where shadows play,
Voices of the ancients sway.
Each step taken, a tale revealed,
Winding whispers, hearts unsealed.

Branches sway with secrets known,
As the path reveals its own.
In the rustle, find your way,
Guided by what spirits say.

Secrets Carried by the Wind

The wind will tell of tales untold,
Secrets wrapped in breezes bold.
Through the branches, softly hum,
A melody of dreams to come.

Carried whispers from afar,
Drawing hearts to where they are.
In its breath, the world confides,
Mysteries that the heart abides.

Musings in the Twilight's Grip

Shadows dance upon the ground,
Silent thoughts, a whispered sound.
Echoes fading, light slips low,
In twilight's grip, the dreams can grow.

Time stands still, the world feels vast,
Moments linger, shadows cast.
In the hush, reflections bloom,
Beneath the twilight's velvet gloom.

Cradles of the Absent Light.

Beneath the stars, the night unfolds,
A cradle where the silence holds.
Absent light, a gentle sway,
In dreams of dusk, we drift away.

Echoes of a day long past,
In this hushed embrace, we cast.
Flickers of hope, a soft refrain,
In shadows deep, like gentle rain.

Whispers in the Twilight

Whispers weave through evening's veil,
As day and night begin to pale.
Stars awaken, soft and bright,
Illuminating paths of night.

In the stillness, secrets sigh,
Echoes of the day gone by.
Every breeze a tale retold,
In twilight's arms, the night unfolds.

Echoes from the Past

Time travels slow, a gentle bend,
Echoes linger, messages send.
Memories wrapped in soft embrace,
In twilight's glow, we find our place.

Faint whispers of what came before,
In shadows deep, we seek for more.
Every heartbeat a story shared,
In twilight's grasp, we are ensnared.

Envelopes of Unnamed Places

In corners where shadows dwell,
Whispers of secrets softly swell.
Maps drawn on the skin of night,
Mysteries wrapped in silver light.

Streets forged from forgotten dreams,
Flowing like water, they weave in streams.
Each step taken, a story unfolds,
In the silence, the unseen calls.

Among the ruins, laughter hides,
In the air, an ancient tide.
Footprints linger, then fade away,
Echoes of lives that chose to stay.

Unraveled threads of fate entwined,
A canvas where lost hearts aligned.
In envelopes of silence, we find,
The essence of places left behind.

Requiem for the Unseen

Softly the night begins to weep,
For shadows and dreams that dared to sleep.
In the silence, a requiem plays,
For those who walk in hidden ways.

Lost in the folds of time's embrace,
Flickers of light leave no trace.
Voices once vibrant, now dimmed, fade,
As echoes of yearning in stillness wade.

Characters woven in twilight's song,
As if the world knew they belonged.
Each heartbeat a memory, bittersweet,
A dance of the unseen, bittersweet.

And in the distance, a bell will toll,
For the unseen, they echo the soul.
In the shadows, a soft goodbye,
A requiem whispered beneath the sky.

The Tapestry of Hidden Voices

Woven threads of whispered tales,
In the silence, the spirit sails.
Colors blend in the softest hue,
Each fiber sings of me and you.

The loom of life, it blends so fine,
Where every stitch becomes a sign.
Voices rise in a vibrant thread,
Stories of those who came and fled.

Within the fabric, secrets hide,
Waves of memories in currents glide.
Unseen hands shape the woven art,
Gathered whispers that touch the heart.

A tapestry rich, yet soft and light,
Blending shadows, embracing night.
In the quiet, the stories merge,
A symphony where souls converge.

Labyrinths of Memory's Touch

In corridors lined with stillness, lost,
Whispers trace paths of memories cost.
Each turn held a secret, a trace,
In labyrinths forged from time and space.

Echoes of laughter, now just a sound,
In the twists and turns, hope can be found.
Bound by the threads that once were spun,
The past dances softly, never done.

Fog drapes the dawn, a spectral view,
As shadows guide thoughts back anew.
Each step taken, a journey unfolds,
Through the corridors, the heart beholds.

In the dim light where dreams reside,
Memories linger, they do not hide.
In the labyrinth's hold, we cling and clutch,
Finding solace in memory's touch.

Lurking in the Liminal Space

A whisper floats in twilight's glow,
Where dreams and daylight cease to flow.
Ghostly figures weave through the mist,
In this place where shadows twist.

Time dances on the fragile thread,
Echoes of what was once said.
A fragile bridge 'twixt here and there,
Lurking whispers fill the air.

In the pause between each breath,
Where silence thrives, and echoes fess.
Footsteps echo, but none are seen,
In liminal space, a haunting sheen.

With every glance, a flicker fades,
Through the veil, reality wades.
What lies beyond the twilight's trace,
Is it fear, or an embrace in space?

Shadows Beneath the Surface

Beneath the waters, secrets dwell,
In depths where shadows spin their spell.
Whispers call from the brackish tide,
A murky world where dreams confide.

Flickers of light dance on the sand,
Ghostly forms shift, yet not a hand.
Silence reigns, but the heartbeats drum,
Shadows watch as the surface hums.

Diving deeper, into the unknown,
Dark waters hold what can't be shown.
Every wave conceals a tale,
Of lives once lived, of hopes set sail.

Searching for what lies under blue,
In the abyss, another view.
Resonating with untold fears,
Shadows bear witness, washed in tears.

The Haunting of Half-remembered Places

In corners where the dust collects,
Whispers linger, soft respects.
Faded echoes call from the past,
In half-remembered spaces cast.

Dilapidated walls conceal,
Stories lost, yet they feel real.
Each creak and crack speaks of despair,
A haunting presence lingers there.

Broken windows, gardens wild,
Where ghosts of youth, forever mild.
Familiar scents of time once stayed,
In these places fondly laid.

A photograph, a smile so clear,
A specter whispers: 'I was here.'
In half-remembered dreams we trace,
The haunting of a cherished place.

Flickering Lights in the Abyss

In the void where silence reigns,
Flickering lights break through the stains.
A glimmer here, a shimmer there,
In shadows deep, they seem to care.

Each pulse a beacon, drawing near,
Hope emerges from the fear.
A dance of sparks in darkened skies,
Where whispering echoes softly rise.

What lies beyond the glowing spheres?
Lonely wishes, silent tears.
Flickers guide the lost and brave,
In the abyss, darkness gave.

With every glow, a story speaks,
In whispered tones, the heartache peaks.
Flickering lights, though soon to cease,
In the abyss, they yield a peace.

The Silence Between Us

In the space where shadows play,
Words unspoken drift away.
Hearts entwined yet far apart,
Silence echoes in the heart.

Beneath the moon's gentle glow,
Unseen paths where dreams may flow.
Eyes that meet but seldom speak,
In stillness, souls feel weak.

Memories linger in the air,
Lingering doubts, a silent prayer.
Time stands still, a fleeting chance,
In shared silence, a longing dance.

Yet hope whispers through the night,
A promise held in distant light.
Together drawn, though miles apart,
In the silence, beats one heart.

Faint Traces in the Dark

In twilight's mist, we leave our mark,
Faint traces whisper in the dark.
Echoes of laughter, soft and low,
Time's gentle hand begins to slow.

Among the stars, secrets confide,
Lost in shadows, we tend to hide.
Each passing moment, tender, bright,
Guiding us through the cool night.

Lost in dreams, where hope takes flight,
Faint traces lead to morning light.
Weaving tales of love and grace,
In the dark, we find our place.

These whispers weave through the night air,
Gentle echoes of love and care.
Faint traces, soft as a sigh,
In the dark, we learn to fly.

Nightfall's Embrace

When night descends with gentle grace,
Stars awaken in their place.
The world is hushed, a tranquil scene,
In night's embrace, we dream unseen.

Moonlit paths and shadows play,
Guiding hearts that drift away.
Softest sighs in stillness breathe,
In night's embrace, we find reprieve.

Whispers linger in the cool air,
Every heartbeat, a silent prayer.
Moments held under the sky,
In night's embrace, we learn to fly.

Together lost in time's sweet flow,
Where dreams are sown and love can grow.
Nightfall's embrace, a tender touch,
In the quiet, we feel so much.

Hushed Whispers of Worlds Apart

In distant realms, where dreams collide,
Hushed whispers echo, worlds divide.
Like distant stars that brightly gleam,
In silence, we awaken dreams.

Voices carried on the breeze,
Fleeting moments, hearts at ease.
Lost in thoughts of what could be,
In whispered hopes, we find the key.

Though miles stretch between our hearts,
In quiet moments, life imparts.
Every glance, a secret shared,
In hushed whispers, love declared.

Across the void, a bond remains,
In silent strength, love's quiet veins.
Hushed whispers will always find,
The way to bridge the ties that bind.

Beneath the Surface of Dreams

Whispers float on twilight air,
Beneath the surface, dreams lay bare.
Shadows dance in silver light,
Holding secrets of the night.

Waves of thought in silence drift,
Glimmers of hope in every rift.
Suspended worlds await the dawn,
Where all fears are gently drawn.

Yet Another Daydream

Beneath the azure skies so bright,
A fleeting thought takes wing in flight.
Moments flash like shooting stars,
Painted dreams beneath the bars.

Softly whispered wishes hum,
Inviting echoes, yet they come.
Drifting close, then out of reach,
Life's lessons quietly teach.

The Sigh of Hidden Valleys

In valleys deep, the silence breathes,
A quiet sigh beneath the leaves.
Nature's hush, a soft embrace,
Cradles time in gentle grace.

Mist envelops the morning light,
Where shadows linger, day and night.
Secrets held in greens and browns,
Whispers soft in leafy crowns.

Murky Waters of Reminiscence

In murky waters, memories swirl,
Fragments of a distant world.
Reflections twisted, hard to see,
Echoes of what used to be.

Fading faces, laughter lost,
A river flows, yet at what cost?
Time's embrace, both warm and cold,
Shadows of stories still untold.

Breaths of Invisible Light

In shadows soft, where dreams take flight,
A whisper glows, a spark so bright.
Unseen currents weave the air,
Carrying hopes, a silent prayer.

Through the dark, a flicker dances,
Glimmers of magic, fleeting chances.
Embers trace a secret path,
Guiding souls to wake from wrath.

In the stillness, moments bloom,
Illuminating corners, banishing gloom.
Each breath a thread, a gentle pull,
Woven stories, deep and full.

With every glow, the heart ignites,
Breaths of joy, in silent nights.
Invisible light, forever near,
A reminder that love conquers fear.

The Weight of Forgotten Stories

Dusty pages, tales untold,
Whispers of heroes, brave and bold.
In echoes lost, their voices fade,
Memories linger, unafraid.

Burdened hearts with dreams that soar,
Beneath the rubble, legends roar.
Each tear shed, a chapter closed,
The weight of life, in ink enclosed.

Fragments cling, a bittersweet song,
Yearning for where they belong.
In silence, the past softly stirs,
Awakening voices, the soul concurs.

Beneath the surface, stories sigh,
In the quiet, they will not die.
The weight they bear, a treasure deep,
In the hearts of those who keep.

Beyond the Misty Veil

Veils of gray, the dawn unwinds,
Hints of magic, fate entwined.
Through the fog, a world anew,
Whispers call, inviting you.

Secrets dance on silver streams,
Reality bleeds into dreams.
With gentle steps, I seek the light,
Beyond the mist, a glorious sight.

Colors paint the silent ether,
Voices rise, a soft hymn bequeather.
In the hush, hope takes its stand,
A promise held in nature's hand.

Through the blur, our hearts align,
Bound by the threads of space and time.
Beyond the veil, our spirits play,
In the warmth of a new day.

Treads on Timeless Roads

Worn and winding, paths we trace,
Marking time in gentle grace.
With every step, memories swell,
Stories woven, in silence dwell.

Underneath the ancient trees,
Whispers flutter in the breeze.
Each footfall echoes tales of old,
Of courage and dreams, brightly bold.

Beneath the stars, we walk as one,
Where shadows merge, and fears come undone.
The roads we tread, both near and far,
Lead us home, no matter where we are.

With every journey, a piece we find,
Bridges build, hearts intertwined.
On timeless roads, we dance and sway,
In the warmth of night, we find our way.

Enchanted Whispers of Time

In the twilight glow, shadows dance,
Echoes of laughter, a fleeting chance.
Softly they weave, tales from the past,
Moments of magic, forever to last.

Time drips like rain from a withered leaf,
Stirring the heart with gentle grief.
Whispers of ages, secrets unfold,
Stories retold, through eyes of gold.

Winds carry voices across the years,
Shadows of joy and shimmering tears.
Every heartbeat, a mystical rhyme,
In the enchanted whispers of time.

Glances at the Unfamiliar

In the crowd, a fleeting glance,
Two souls connect in a soft dance.
Eyes like windows, secrets reside,
In the air, unspoken tides.

Every stranger holds a story untold,
A world within, waiting to unfold.
Silent moments, a lingering sigh,
A glance exchanged, as time slips by.

Familiarity blooms in the unknown,
Like wildflowers in a field overgrown.
Unfamiliar paths lead to the heart,
Glances that forge, never to part.

Poems Written in the Clouds

Up above where the sky meets dreams,
Clouds weave stories in soft moonbeams.
Puffy whispers dance in the air,
Words of wonder linger everywhere.

A canvas of blue, where imaginations soar,
Each shape transforms, a tale to explore.
With every drift, a new verse is spun,
In the gentle embrace of the rising sun.

Dreamers gaze high, searching for signs,
In the wispy trails, oracular designs.
Poems unfold, delicate and bright,
Written in clouds, a fleeting delight.

Recollections of a Faded Portrait

In a dusty frame, memories lie,
Captured in hues of a soft goodbye.
Eyes that once sparkled, now dimmed with age,
Stories of love penned on a page.

Fingers trace outlines, soft as a sigh,
Echoes of laughter that once filled the sky.
Time drips like wax on forgotten art,
Each brushstroke whispers a longing heart.

Faded colors, but vibrant within,
Recollections of moments where we've been.
In the stillness, the past gently stays,
A faded portrait, where memory plays.

Hues of Distant Echoes

In twilight's grasp, the colors fade,
Whispers of time in silence laid.
Echoes dance on silver streams,
Carrying forth forgotten dreams.

Shadows stretch across the land,
Footsteps lost in shifting sand.
Crimson clouds in evening's fire,
Awaken thoughts of deep desire.

Through twilight's veil, a tale unfolds,
Of love and loss, of truths untold.
Each hue a memory, soft yet bright,
Painting stories in fading light.

Stars will rise, and night will call,
A tapestry woven, binding us all.
In distant echoes, hearts will roam,
Finding solace in the unknown.

Under the Silent Canopy

Beneath the leaves where shadows sigh,
The world departs, and secrets lie.
Branches weave a quiet shroud,
Embracing whispers soft and loud.

Mossy paths where dreams do tread,
Nature's arms cradle the dead.
Softly humming, a breeze will sweep,
Lulling the forest into sleep.

Sunlight filters through the green,
A patchwork quilt of light unseen.
Time stands still under the boughs,
In tranquil peace, the heart allows.

Voices echo, yet none are near,
In the stillness, all becomes clear.
Under the silent canopy,
We find our place, wild and free.

Fragments of a Hidden Realm

In corners dark where shadows dance,
Lies a world alive with chance.
Fragments gleam with a ghostly light,
Drawing forth our hearts to flight.

Echoes bounce between the trees,
Carried softly on the breeze.
Whispers speak of paths untrod,
In hidden realms, where dreams are plod.

Each step reveals a tale unspun,
Of battles fought and races run.
In fragments brief, life's essence flows,
Unseen magic in subtle shows.

Bound by threads of memory's weave,
In this realm, we learn to believe.
With every breath, the heart shall soar,
A hidden realm to explore more.

Murmurs of Unseen Horizons

Beyond the mist, where worlds collide,
Murmurs call from far and wide.
Horizons stretch like dreams in flight,
Drawing the soul toward the light.

Each whisper holds a tale to share,
Of journeys taken, hearts laid bare.
With every dawn, the canvas grows,
A masterpiece, as nature shows.

At dusk, the skies ignite in flame,
Reminding us we're never the same.
In fading light, we find our way,
Murmurs guiding us through the gray.

So let us wander, hearts aflame,
Chasing the echoes of a name.
For unseen horizons call us near,
In whispers soft, we cast our fear.

Flickers of Time's Embrace

In shadows cast by fading light,
A moment whispers, soft and bright.
Time dances lightly on the edge,
Of dreams that linger, hearts that pledge.

The clock unwinds, a tender sigh,
As echoes of our laughter fly.
With every tick, a memory grows,
In flickers where the past bestows.

A sunbeam caught in morning dew,
Reflects the paths we wandered through.
In every pause, a story's spun,
Beneath the gaze of setting sun.

Embrace the now, let moments freeze,
In fleeting breaths, find hearts at ease.
For time's embrace might fade away,
Yet love remains, come what may.

The Resonance of Unheld Hands

In silence speaks the space between,
Two souls adrift, as if unseen.
A glance that lingers, then recedes,
Unheld hands weave unspoken needs.

The echoes of a promise made,
In whispered winds that will not fade.
Each heartbeat thrums a timeless song,
In resonance where two hearts long.

A touch, ungrasped, ignites the air,
With dreams that shimmer everywhere.
Though fingers part, the warmth remains,
In every thought, where love sustains.

In longing's depth, a bridge is cast,
Connecting futures with the past.
Though hands may never softly meet,
Their journey's pulse remains complete.

Beyond the Reach of Memory

With fading hues of evening's glow,
Memories linger, soft and slow.
Beyond the grasp of time's embrace,
A treasure trove, a sacred space.

The flicker of a distant star,
Calls forth the moments, near and far.
Each smile, each tear, a fleeting thread,
Weaving the tales of words unsaid.

In shadows cast by memory's light,
Old echoes dance in silent night.
We chase the whispers of the past,
Yet hold them close, as shadows last.

For in the heart where love remains,
Beyond the reach, no loss contains.
Each fleeting glimpse, each soft refrain,
In timelessness, we meet again.

The Pulse of Distant Worlds

In cosmic swirls of dark and light,
A pulse resounds, both swift and bright.
With every heartbeat of the night,
Distant worlds beckon, taking flight.

Stars align in patterns vast,
Whispering secrets from the past.
Across the void, a song is sung,
Of journeys endless, yet so young.

Galaxies spin, a twinkling dream,
In the silence, a vivid stream.
The pulse of life in endless flow,
Unfolds the mysteries we long to know.

So let us gaze into the skies,
With wonder etched in hopeful eyes.
For every heartbeat, every spark,
Connects us all, ignites the dark.

Lurking Beyond the Fading Sun

Shadows stretch as day concedes,
Whispers ride the evening breeze.
Beneath the twilight's gentle sigh,
Mysteries of night draw nigh.

Veils of dusk, secrets swirled,
Crafting tales of a hidden world.
Footfalls echo on the ground,
In the dark, solace is found.

Time wavers as pale stars bloom,
While the moon casts its soft gloom.
A beckoning call from the deep,
Where the restless shadows creep.

Lurking figures, soft and shy,
Beneath the watchful, starlit sky.
Through the night, spirits roam,
Searching for a place called home.

Silhouettes of the Untraveled Path

Beneath the arch of ancient trees,
Where roots twist in the hushed breeze.
Footprints lost to time's embrace,
Trace the lines of a forgotten place.

Every turn hides tales untold,
Of adventurers brave and bold.
Silhouettes dance in shadows deep,
Guarding secrets they must keep.

The path unwinds in whispers low,
Where only the brave dare to go.
In the stillness, echoes call,
Inviting wanderers to enthrall.

Mysteries woven in moonlit threads,
Await the dreams that fill our heads.
With each step, the heart takes flight,
On the untraveled path of night.

Starlit Dreamscapes of Yore

In the quiet of the midnight glow,
Dreams weave soft as rivers flow.
Above, the stars begin to sing,
Revealing tales of everything.

Whispers of an age gone by,
Float like clouds in the boundless sky.
Visions dance like fireflies bright,
Painting the canvas of the night.

Each constellation a story shared,
Of heroes lost, of souls laid bare.
In every twinkle, history glows,
Mysteries deep in the cosmos flows.

Dreamscapes where the heart can soar,
In unity with the stars of yore.
Let the night cradle your thoughts,
In starlit dreams, hope is sought.

Vagabonds of the Half-Light Realm

In the dusk where shadows blend,
Vagabonds wander without an end.
With whispers of the night they roam,
Searching for a place called home.

Half-light wraps them in a shroud,
Lost among the drifting crowd.
Stories linger in their eyes,
Echoes of laughter, soft goodbyes.

On borrowed time, they tread the line,
Between the worlds, they intertwine.
Windswept dreams in the twilight's song,
Guide their steps where they belong.

Each heart carries a weight untold,
A treasure chest of hopes and gold.
Through the night, they seek and find,
The magic woven in the mind.

Allure of the Uncharted Depths

In the heart of the sea, where whispers dwell,
Secrets lie buried, casting their spell.
Colors of coral in vibrant embrace,
Life dances gracefully, a silent space.

Bubbles rise softly, a melodic tune,
Drawing explorers beneath the bright moon.
Gentle waves beckon with tales of old,
Mysteries waiting, treasures of gold.

In the shadows, the creatures glide,
Silent observers of the ocean's wide tide.
Curiosity sparks in the dark abyss,
Every movement a promise, a chance not to miss.

With each stroke of the fin, dreams intertwine,
In the depths of the blue, the soul can align.
A journey unending, horizons that call,
In the watery world, where the heart learns to fall.

Twilight's Embrace on Lost Journeys

As the sun bows down, the skies are aglow,
Shadows stretch long, signaling the slow.
Whispers of twilight in colors so warm,
Guiding the wanderers through every form.

Paths underfoot, lined with old stones,
Each step a memory, each echo atones.
Silhouettes dance in the fading light,
Chasing the dreams that unravel the night.

The air grows cooler, with secrets it shares,
Stories of travelers, dreams, and their glares.
Stars break the silence with twinkling eyes,
In the depths of shadows, the future lies.

In twilight's embrace, so fragile, so sweet,
Journeys are forged where lost spirits meet.
With every heartbeat, a promise anew,
In the embrace of dusk, all dreams can come true.

Echoing Footfalls of the Past

On cobblestone pathways, history breathes,
Whispers of footsteps, where memory weaves.
Faded reflections in twilight's dim glow,
Echoes of laughter, the tales that we know.

Every corner turned holds fragments of old,
Locked in the silence, their stories unfold.
Time paints the walls with the brush of regret,
Yet hopes of tomorrow are never upset.

A flicker of candles lights up the dark,
Guiding the souls who once left their mark.
In the corridors echoing with sighs,
There lie the moments that never say goodbye.

Through windows half-open, the breeze carries near,
Soft murmurs of voices we wish we could hear.
In the gallery of time, dreams long amassed,
We walk hand in hand with the echoes of past.

Whims of the Enigmatic Night

Beneath the soft veil of the star-studded sky,
Whispers of dreams and the moon's gentle sigh.
Mysterious shadows glimmer and play,
As the night weaves its magic, holding sway.

Crickets serenade with their rhythmic song,
Tales of adventure where wanderers long.
Each breeze carries secrets, soft and profound,
In the depths of the dark, a beauty unbound.

In silvered reflections of the still pond's face,
The night holds enchantment in delicate grace.
Every heartbeat syncs with the cosmos above,
As we surrender to the night's gentle love.

Lost in the allure of the mystical dark,
The whispers of night ignite a bold spark.
With every breath taken under the stars' glow,
We dance on the edge where the wild dreams flow.

Secrets of the Unseen Realm

Whispers dance on twilight's breeze,
Hidden paths beneath the trees.
Shadows weave a silent tale,
Magic breathes where dreams prevail.

Mysteries in silence lie,
Glimmers caught in a passing sigh.
Stars above, a watchful gaze,
Guiding hearts through twilight's haze.

In the quiet, secrets grow,
Planting seeds of what we know.
With every step, the veils unfold,
Revealing wonders yet untold.

Embrace the night, let visions soar,
Through hidden realms, we seek and explore.
The unseen whispers softly call,
In shadows deep, we find it all.

Reflections in the Dusk

The sun dips low, a golden hue,
Painting skies with shades anew.
Memories swirl in fading light,
Capturing moments, soft and bright.

Echoes linger in the air,
Whispers of a time laid bare.
Shadows stretch, the day does wane,
As silence wraps the world in gain.

Stillness falls, the night is near,
In twilight's glow, we hold what's dear.
Reflections dance upon the stream,
Carrying forth each faded dream.

In dusk's embrace, hearts find their peace,
From everyday worries, a sweet release.
A tranquil pause, a gentle sigh,
In the embrace of the twilight sky.

Hints of a Forgotten Landscape

Beneath the overgrowth lies a story,
Of ancient trails and lost glory.
Whispers of woods once vibrant and grand,
Now fading dreams, a quiet land.

Echoes of laughter in rustling leaves,
The sigh of time through the autumn eaves.
Stones speak softly of days long past,
While wildflowers bloom, free and vast.

Sunlight dapples the forest floor,
In every corner, a tale to explore.
Hints of the past in shadows cast,
A forgotten scene where memories last.

Nature's palette, rich and deep,
Holds secrets of those who once did weep.
In silence, the echoes still remain,
Of a landscape lost to time's sweet refrain.

Murmurs from the Other Side

Voices linger where shadows blend,
Soft secrets that the night does send.
In quiet moments, they call to me,
Murmurs whispering, setting me free.

Across the veil, the warmth resides,
Hints of laughter where light abides.
Lost souls wander in peaceful grace,
Tracing paths in a gentle embrace.

Through the silence, a soft refrain,
Promising hope amidst the pain.
In every heart, a story penned,
Each murmur a bridge, each spirit a friend.

So here I stand, attuned and awake,
Listening closely for love's sweet stake.
Murmurs from beyond softly guide,
In shadows where the heart won't hide.

Whispers from Forgotten Corners

In shadows deep, the secrets lie,
Soft murmurs call as time slips by.
Old memories dance in quiet grace,
The past awakens in this narrow space.

Flickering lights in the weary night,
Ghostly figures come to share their plight.
Echoes of laughter, a fleeting sound,
In forgotten corners, they still abound.

The walls have ears, they listen close,
To every heart that dare expose.
Whispers blend with the autumn breeze,
Carrying tales with effortless ease.

So linger here, where time stands still,
Embrace the shivers, the quiet thrill.
For in these echoes, we find our way,
Through whispers, past shadows, into the day.

Echoes in the Twilight Vale

In twilight's glow, the world turns soft,
Whispers of night begin to waft.
Beneath the stars, the secrets plead,
As dreams arise from the ancient reed.

Footsteps echo on the mossy ground,
Lost spirits wander, but never found.
Through shadowed paths where shadows play,
Time suspends in the fading gray.

Rippling streams hum a gentle tune,
The air is thick with the scent of June.
Winds carry stories from long ago,
In twilight vale, where soft hearts glow.

Remembered in whispers, long gone days,
Echoes entwine in a wistful haze.
In this quietude, we can discover,
The beating pulse of each hidden lover.

Veils of Gloom Beneath the Stars

Under veils of night, shadows conspire,
Silent secrets clothed in fire.
The stars bear witness to what remains,
In every heart, the thread of chains.

Gloom wraps tight like a lover's sigh,
Whispers of sorrow drift and fly.
Faint glimmers shine through layers thick,
As dreams are shattered with a haunting flick.

Beneath the stars, the night can weep,
For all the hopes that we can't keep.
But in the darkness, there's also grace,
A fragile beauty in that vast space.

So tread softly on this haunted land,
For every shadow holds a hand.
As veils of gloom can softly part,
Revealing light within the heart.

Footprints in the Dim Light

In dim light's glow, the path unfolds,
Stories untold in silence mold.
Footprints linger upon the earth,
Marking the places of fleeting worth.

Each step a whisper, a life once lived,
Fragments of joy, of dreams perceived.
Beneath the weight of the moon's soft gaze,
Footprints dance in a gentle phase.

Shadows grow long as day retreats,
Echoes of laughter linger in beats.
Through every inch of this winding road,
Memories left that time bestowed.

So wander on with an open heart,
In every stride, there's a brand new start.
For every footprint, a story flows,
In the dim light's embrace, our journey grows.

Silent Footsteps in the Night

The moonlight casts a silver glow,
As shadows dance, and spirits flow.
Whispers echo through the trees,
Carried softly on the breeze.

Each sound a secret held so tight,
In the quiet of the night.
Footsteps wander, soft and slow,
In the realm where dreamers go.

Crickets sing their lullaby,
While the stars begin to sigh.
Time stands still in twilight's hush,
As moments blend into a rush.

The night conceals both joy and pain,
In its embrace, we feel the strain.
Yet in silence, hope ignites,
Guiding souls through shadowed nights.

Faded Memories on the Breeze

Whispers of laughter, echoes of old,
Stories of warmth in the crisp air told.
Faded photographs, a life now past,
Drift like leaves on the breeze so fast.

Time paints over with colors dim,
Moments once bright now grow so thin.
Yet in the heart, they softly remain,
A gentle reminder of joy and pain.

Each gust carries a scent of the past,
Mingling memories that forever last.
A child's sweet laughter, a lover's sigh,
Residing softly as days pass by.

In the dance of the wind, they intertwine,
Faded memories, like olden wine.
Sipped slowly in the quiet of night,
Through the whispers, we find our light.

Between the Lines of Existence

In the margins where dreams reside,
They whisper truths we often hide.
Between each line, a heartbeat's song,
A journey where we all belong.

Life's narrative, carved in fate,
We write our story, contemplate.
Moments woven, thread by thread,
In the silence, words left unsaid.

The space between, a canvas bare,
Colors emerge, feelings laid there.
Each pause, a chance for us to breathe,
To find the meaning that we believe.

So read the silence, seek what's true,
Between the lines, discover you.
In every heartbeat, every sigh,
Existence calls us to fly high.

The Compass of Forgotten Choices

Paths diverged in moments past,
Each decision, a die was cast.
A compass points, yet feels so vague,
In the shadows where doubts plague.

Lost in the maze of paths untaken,
Echoes of dreams that now feel shaken.
Each choice a marker on time's grand map,
Yet here we stand, caught in the gap.

What ifs linger like whispers low,
In the heart where regrets can grow?
Yet still the compass spins its way,
Guiding us through the night and day.

For every choice, a lesson learned,
Through the flames, our spirits burned.
We navigate with heart and soul,
Finding peace as we become whole.

Ghost Towns of the Heart

Silent whispers linger near,
Echoes of those once held dear.
Empty roads where laughter played,
Memories in shadows fade.

Windows cracked and doors ajar,
Faded signs of who we are.
Footsteps tracing paths of loss,
In this town we bear our cross.

Dusty streets, achingly bare,
Lonely hearts that did once share.
Silent cries in the moon's glow,
Love's ghost still haunts below.

In the quiet, hope must strive,
Finding ways to feel alive.
In these ruins, love still yearns,
Ghost towns fade, but still it burns.

The Crossroads of Longing

Two paths meet in twilight's hue,
One of dreams, the other true.
At this fork, my heart must choose,
In the silence, which to lose?

Every step a weight to bear,
Questions linger in the air.
Hope and fear, they intertwine,
At this moment, will I shine?

Voices call from paths unseen,
Whispers soft, yet oh so keen.
In this place of choice and strife,
I search for meaning in my life.

Crossroads often bring the pain,
Yet from sorrow, joy can reign.
With each turn, the heart must trust,
Finding peace is always a must.

Eclipsed by Time's Hand

Time slips past like grains of sand,
Moments fade, we cannot stand.
Memories drown in shadows cast,
Fleeting echoes of the past.

As shadows stretch into the night,
Hope flickers, dimming light.
Each heartbeat, a gentle sigh,
Whispers of the days gone by.

We chase dreams that slip away,
In the dark where memories play.
Yet, through the dark, a spark can rise,
Illuminating hidden skies.

Though eclipsed, the light remains,
In the heart, love still sustains.
Through the void, we find our way,
Time can't steal what hearts convey.

Sifting Through the Dust of Yesterday

In the remnants, pieces lie,
Dust of dreams that kissed the sky.
Looking back, I start to sift,
Treasures found, a quiet gift.

Photos faded, stories told,
Echoes of the days of old.
Tender moments whisper soft,
In the dust, memories loft.

Each grain holds a world of light,
Lessons learned from day to night.
Through the haze, a gentle guide,
In the past, love must abide.

Sifting through what once has been,
Finding joy in what's unseen.
Though the dust may settle low,
In yesterday, love still flows.

In the Realm of Quiet Longing

Whispers of dusk linger low,
Hearts entwined in shadows' glow.
Promises lost in the night air,
Yearning souls, a fragile prayer.

Stars blink softly, dreams take flight,
Memory dances in the light.
Fingers trace the silent space,
Echoes fill the empty place.

Hope resides where silence breathes,
Time holds secrets, gently weaves.
Through the dark, a spark ignites,
Longing thrives in starry nights.

Flickers of Another Time

In the shadows of the past,
Moments flicker, memories cast.
Every smile, a fleeting glimpse,
Joyful laughter, like soft chimes.

Candles burn with stories told,
Dreams and wishes, pure as gold.
A child's laugh, a mother's sigh,
Echoing where the heart might lie.

Through the lens of faded days,
Light refracts in gentle ways.
Old photographs, a silent muse,
Time whispers softly, never lose.

Illusions Beneath the Moon

Beneath the silvery, soft gleam,
Shadows weave a haunting dream.
Branches sway with whispered lore,
Veils of night, they softly pour.

Stars like jewels in velvet skies,
Craft illusions from our sighs.
Dance of echoes, fleeting grace,
Hearts entwined in twilight's embrace.

Mirrors crack under the light,
Reflections blur, day turns to night.
In the stillness, secrets bloom,
Unravel truths through the looming gloom.

Footprints on the Edge of Reality

Footprints tread on sands of dreams,
Lost amid the moonlit beams.
Waves crash softly, time reclaims,
Fleeting moments, whispered names.

On the verge of what is real,
Minds explore, hearts start to feel.
The horizon blurs, colors merge,
Endless paths, a constant surge.

Thoughts like shadows, drift and sway,
Guide the heart to find its way.
In this space of pause and doubt,
Truth reveals what life's about.

Fantasies of the Obscured Horizon

In twilight's grasp, dreams softly weave,
Whispers of worlds that dusk conceives.
Shadows dance on the edge of light,
Crafting visions, a wondrous sight.

Echoes of laughter in the still air,
Hints of adventures we long to share.
Stars will guide with a silken thread,
Mapping the paths where our hopes are led.

Restless spirits float on the breeze,
Unlocking tales beneath ancient trees.
Mysteries linger where shadows play,
In the realm where night conquers day.

A tapestry woven with passion and fear,
Chasing horizons that draw ever near.
Each fleeting moment, a flickering flame,
In the heart of the dreamer, igniting the same.

Trails through the Mystic Mists

Through veils of fog, pathways unfold,
Stories of journeys, both young and old.
Silhouettes whisper in the cloak of night,
Guiding lost souls with ethereal light.

Animals tread on the damp, soft ground,
In the silence, an echoing sound.
Each step we take, a promise made,
In the heart of the mist, shadows parade.

The air is thick with secrets and sighs,
Beneath the blanket of starlit skies.
Mysterious forces pull us along,
Where the soul finds comfort, and dreams belong.

A realm untouched by the hands of time,
In every corner, a rhythm, a rhyme.
Through trails of the mystic, we wander, we roam,
In the warmth of the fog, we find our home.

Clarity in the Veiled Abyss

In depths unexplored, the darkness brews,
Questions rippling through the ominous hues.
Yet from the shadows, a heartbeat sings,
Whispers of truth that the silence brings.

Beneath the surface, chaos takes form,
Fleeting glimpses of the calm before storm.
Each tear that falls is a crystal clear,
Reflecting realities we try to steer.

The veiled abyss holds secrets untold,
Yet in its core, a warmth that's bold.
Navigating depths with courage in hand,
Finding our way to a safer land.

Clarity blooms like a flower in night,
Turning the fears into sheer delight.
Out of the darkness, into the light,
From the abyss, our spirits take flight.

Voices of the Beneath

From depths of the earth, a chorus arises,
Soft murmurings weave through ancient surprises.
Echoes of wisdom, the wise ones share,
In the heart of the silence, we surrender and bare.

Fables of old in the cracks of the stone,
Secrets locked in the bones that have grown.
Whispers of life, of loss, and of love,
Carry the dreams to the heavens above.

Voices entwined with the rustling leaves,
In harmony sung, the spirit retrieves.
Each gentle sound is a message sent,
Connecting the past with the present intent.

In twilight's embrace, we listen and hear,
The truths of the earth that linger near.
With each passing breath, the stories take flight,
The voices of beneath, in the hush of the night.

Veils of Forgotten Dreams

In the shadows, whispers sigh,
Lost within the night's soft cry.
A tapestry of hopes once spun,
Underneath the veils, they run.

Echoes of laughter linger near,
Fleeting moments, now unclear.
Winds of time blow gentle grief,
Carrying the lost belief.

Flickers dance in twilight's hue,
Memories bathed in silver dew.
Catch the spark, feel the glow,
In veils of dreams, we ebb and flow.

Yet as dawn breaks, shadows flee,
Revealing hearts that long to see.
Whispers fade but won't erase,
The beauty held in time's embrace.

Secrets of the Starlit Path

Upon a trail where shadows play,
Secrets linger, night turns day.
Stars like lanterns guide my way,
In silent whispers, dreams convey.

Footsteps hushed on ancient stone,
Echoes of a fate unknown.
With every step, the heart does yearn,
For mysteries that twist and turn.

Moonlight spills like liquid gold,
Stories of the brave and bold.
Each glimmer holds a tale untold,
Beneath the stars, we break the mold.

Through these woods, where silence reigns,
Secrets woven through the veins.
In every breeze, they circle back,
On starlit paths, there's no lack.

Gossamer Veils of Memory

Threads of time, so fine and bright,
Gossamer veils in morning light.
They catch the hues of joy and pain,
A tapestry of loss and gain.

Fleeting moments, soft and sweet,
Dance like leaves at autumn's feet.
In the quiet, echoes call,
Remnants of the rise and fall.

Through wisps of dreams that intertwine,
We find the truths that brightly shine.
A fragile world of what has been,
We hold it close, the kindness seen.

Yet as the sunset bids goodbye,
Memories linger, never die.
In gossamer veils, they softly dwell,
In the heart's chambers, all is well.

Chasing Faint Reflections

In pools of water, shadows play,
Chasing echoes of the day.
Faint reflections of what's past,
Moments slipping, fading fast.

Ripples form with every breath,
Life and laughter, love and death.
Glimmers trapped in liquid space,
A dance of time, a fleeting grace.

We reach for visions hard to grasp,
In silver light, memories clasp.
Through whispered dreams, we wander free,
Chasing reflections, yearning to see.

Yet dawn will break, and shadows close,
Leaving only the heart's prose.
In chasing glimpses of what's real,
We find the truths that fate reveals.

Enigma of the Echoing Darkness

In shadows deep, secrets play,
Whispers linger, night and day.
Ghostly echoes call my name,
A dance of silence, fierce and tame.

Moonlight weaves through branches bare,
Veiling thoughts that wander where.
Darkness sings a haunting tune,
In the depths, lost hopes commune.

Mysteries in the midnight air,
Veiled in silence, dreams laid bare.
With every breath, I delve inside,
In the enigma, darkness hides.

A flicker faint, a fleeting spark,
Guides the way through realms so dark.
In the echo, I find my place,
Embraced by night, a warm embrace.

Twilight's Quiet Serenade

The sun dips low, a soft goodbye,
Colors blend in the painted sky.
Whispers of dusk caress the air,
A tranquil song beyond compare.

Stars awaken, twinkling bright,
Casting dreams on the veil of night.
As shadows dance in gentle sway,
Twilight hums its sweet ballet.

Beneath the boughs, the nightbirds sing,
Each note a promise, soft as spring.
In the afterglow, hearts align,
Time slows down, the world is fine.

With every breath, a moment's grace,
In twilight's arms, we find our space.
Embraced by peace, we softly tread,
In the quiet, our spirits wed.

The Language of Silent Reflections

In stillness lies a world profound,
Where thoughts take shape without a sound.
Mirrored surfaces, secrets shared,
In silence, every heart laid bare.

Ripples dance on a tranquil pool,
Reflecting dreams, the past a jewel.
Words unspoken, deep insights gleaned,
In quietude, the heart is screened.

Eyes like windows, souls unfold,
Tales of warmth, both meek and bold.
Each glance a bridge, a language true,
In silence, I find myself in you.

With every pause, a deeper note,
In the quiet, all voices float.
Listen close, the truth in sight,
In silent depths, we find the light.

Rooted in Forgotten Paths

Old trees whisper tales of yore,
Each ring a story, a memory's door.
Roots entwined in the earth's embrace,
Hold the secrets of time and space.

Veins of history run deep and wide,
In each shadow, ancient dreams abide.
Paths once traveled, now overgrown,
Yet in their midst, we find a home.

Golden leaves fall to the ground,
In their crinkle, lost voices found.
Nature's grip, both fierce and sweet,
Guides the wanderer's wandering feet.

Underneath the endless sky,
Forgotten paths never truly die.
In every step, the past lives on,
Rooted in stories, we are not alone.

Mythos of the Enshrouded Glade

Whispers laced in twilight's glow,
Ancient secrets in shadows flow.
Trees standing tall, a timeless guard,
Nature's tales spoken, never marred.

Moss carpets earth in a vibrant green,
Faeries flicker where none have been.
Under the boughs, dreams intertwine,
Lost in moments, both yours and mine.

The brook babbles low, a song of past,
Echoes of laughter, forever cast.
Sparkling eyes of the creatures shy,
Forever watching, they seek to fly.

In the glade's embrace, time stands still,
Hearts beat softly, with nature's will.
Mythos we weave in whispers of night,
Together we dance in the fading light.

Unfurling the Curtains of the Indiscernible

Veils of dusk enshroud the view,
Allowing glimpses of what is true.
The mind's eye blinks, sights askew,
In shadows deeper, mysteries brew.

Threads of silence weave the dark,
Questions linger, a subtle spark.
Winds carry tales from worlds unknown,
Where whispers thrive, and seeds are sown.

Past the veil, a soft light glows,
Hidden pathways where knowledge flows.
Unraveling fears, we dare to see,
What lies beyond, what could be free.

So let us peel back layers of night,
Together we'll find the hidden light.
In the folds of existence, truth may rise,
Illuminated dreams beneath starlit skies.

Dances in the Fathomless Shade

In twilight's embrace, shadows grow,
An echo of movement, soft and slow.
Beneath the oak, spirits glide,
In silent rhythms, they twist and slide.

Moonlight spills on the forest floor,
A luminous dance, forevermore.
Branches sway with a gentle grace,
While whispers of magic fill the space.

Each twinkle of light, a step in time,
Nature's symphony, pure and sublime.
Mysteries linger in the cool night air,
As shadows whisper secrets rare.

In this realm where wonders await,
We join the dance, surrender fate.
Within the darkness, we feel alive,
In fathomless shade, our spirits thrive.

Reverie of the Invisible Realm

Deep in the mind, where thoughts reside,
A realm unfolds, where dreams abide.
Unseen whispers beckon the soul,
In the silence, we feel whole.

Mirages flash in the corners of sight,
A tapestry woven of day and night.
Echoes guard the paths we tread,
Each thread of vision, softly spread.

In the heart of calm lies a flicker bright,
A flame of hope in the endless night.
Here, we find what cannot be shown,
A treasure of thought, ours alone.

So drift with me through this hidden door,
Into the mist, forevermore.
In the realm of dreams, we'll forever dance,
In reverie's arms, given a chance.

Lost in the Feedback Loop

In shadows deep where echoes dwell,
Thoughts spiral round, a silent bell.
Whispers drown in endless cries,
A maze of sound where reason lies.

Each turn we take, a path unseen,
Chasing dreams that might have been.
Fractured voices blur the night,
In this loop, we lose our sight.

A cycle spins, a fragile thread,
Words unspoken, hopes long dead.
Yet still we seek, with hearts in bloom,
In circles drawn, we find our doom.

Through static haze, a truth we grasp,
Happiness lost in an endless clasp.
Hope flickers dim, yet still we sway,
In the loop, we long to stay.

An Odyssey of Unspoken Words

Between the lines of whispered dreams,
Lies a story stitched at the seams.
Silent echoes dance on lips,
A journey starts with desperate trips.

In shadows cast by doubt and fear,
The weight of silence draws us near.
Navigating through uncharted seas,
Our voices caught in fading breeze.

Each heartbeat holds a tale untold,
An odyssey wrapped in threads of gold.
Beneath the silence, hearts collide,
In the depths where truths abide.

With every glance, a world unfolds,
In a bond stronger than mere holds.
Weaving words, through time we fly,
In unspoken thoughts, we learn to sigh.

Under the Gaze of Distant Stars

Beneath a sky of endless dreams,
Twinkle bright where silence gleams.
A cosmic dance, the stars align,
In their gaze, our spirits entwine.

Wandering paths both near and far,
Guided gently by a lone star.
In every whisper of cosmic dust,
We trace the past and future's trust.

Moments flutter like a comet's tail,
Unraveling stories, a timeless trail.
Bathed in light of celestial art,
We find our place, we make a start.

Each twinkle speaks of hopes and fears,
A symphony hums, the universe hears.
In the night, our souls embrace,
Under the gaze, we find our space.

The Elusiveness of What Was

Memories drift like autumn leaves,
Fleeting whispers the heart retrieves.
Echoes linger, sweet and sore,
A tapestry woven, but frayed at the core.

In the twilight of what once was,
Time's embrace stirs without pause.
Chasing shadows of fading light,
We grapple with the lingering night.

Moments captured in a fragile frame,
Fleeting glances, a forgotten name.
Yet in the dust, a spark may glow,
In the elusiveness, we still grow.

What we've lost, we seek to find,
In the echoes of the heart and mind.
With every breath, we softly sigh,
For in the past, we still rely.

In the Embrace of the Unknown

Where shadows dance and whispers lead,
The heart beats soft, a quiet creed.
In twilight's hush, we take a chance,
To find the light in dark's romance.

The stars above, they seem to call,
With glimmers bright, a cosmic thrall.
Each step we take, a leap of faith,
In paths unknown, we find our wraith.

Through tangled woods and skies of gray,
We'll chase our dreams, come what may.
With every breath, a story spun,
In the embrace of the unknown, we run.

With open hearts, we dare to roam,
For in the vastness, we find our home.
The journey's worth, it's ours to claim,
In the unknown, we'll stake our name.

Chimeras in the Night

In moonlight's glow, illusions play,
With fleeting forms that drift away.
A dance of shadows, soft and bright,
Chimeras twirl in the velvet night.

Each whisper soft, a secret told,
In dreams we weave, both brave and bold.
With every heartbeat, magic blooms,
In echoes found in twilight's rooms.

They haunt our thoughts, yet set us free,
These phantoms born of mystery.
As stardust spirals in the air,
We chase the dreams that shimmer fair.

Through tangled branches, we will run,
Chasing shadows 'til night is done.
In chimeras, we find our flight,
Awakening truth in the heart of night.

The Curvature of Lost Moments

Time bends and sways like gentle streams,
With fleeting thoughts and fragile dreams.
In each embrace, a whisper lost,
We trace the past, no matter the cost.

Through subtle lines on weathered hands,
We gather tales from distant lands.
Embarked on journeys never whole,
In centuries worn, we seek our soul.

The weight of seconds in the air,
Each memory lingers, rich and rare.
In quiet corners, echoes stay,
The curvature of lost moments sway.

A soft reminder as we flee,
In all that was, we dare to see.
Through stories etched in time's embrace,
We search for solace in our place.

Broken Time in a Crystal Jar

Fragments twinkle, caught in glass,
Each moment frozen, none shall pass.
A glimpse of past, a tearful sigh,
In crystal jars where memories lie.

Ticking softly, the clock it mocks,
While futures wait and tumble blocks.
The heart beats wild, a curious beat,
In broken time, we find our seat.

Held tightly close, we dare to save,
The fleeting joys, memories brave.
As time drips down like sand from hand,
In the jar of dreams, we make our stand.

So let it shatter; let shards unfold,
For in each piece, a story told.
In broken time, we find our way,
In the crystal jar, we choose to stay.

Milton Keynes UK
Ingram Content Group UK Ltd.
UKHW022005131124
451149UK00013B/1017